LIVY

HANNIBAL'S CROSSING OF THE ALPS

TRANSLATED BY AUBREY DE SÉLINCOURT

PENGUIN BOOKS

PENGUIN BOOKS

Published by the Penguin Group
Penguin Books Ltd, 27 Wrights Lane, London w8 5tz, England
Penguin Books USA Inc., 375 Hudson Street, New York, New York, 10014, USA
Penguin Books Australia Ltd, Ringwood, Victoria, Australia
Penguin Books Canada Ltd, 10 Alcorn Avenue, Toronto, Ontario, Canada m4v 3b2
Penguin Books (NZ) Ltd, 182–190 Wairau Road, Auckland 10, New Zealand

Penguin Books Ltd, Registered Offices: Harmondsworth, Middlesex, England

These extracts are from Aubrey de Sélincourt's translation of
The War with Hannibal by Livy, first published in Penguin Classics 1965
This edition published 1995
1   3   5   7   9   10   8   6   4   2

Filmset by Datix International Limited, Bungay, Suffolk
Printed in England by Clays Ltd, St Ives plc

Hannibal's Crossing of the Alps

After the capture of Saguntum Hannibal had retired to winter quarters in New Carthage. News was brought him of the various activities in Rome and Carthage and of the decisions which had been made, so when he learned that he was himself the cause of the coming war as well as the commander-in-chief of the Carthaginian armies, he determined to act swiftly. As soon as he had completed the division and sale of the remainder of the captured material, he summoned a meeting of his Spanish troops, and addressed them as follows: 'My friends, no doubt you see as well as I do that, with all the Spanish peoples subject to our influence, one of two courses is open to us: either we must stop fighting and disband our armies, or pursue our conquests elsewhere. By doing the latter, and by seeking plunder and renown from the conquest of other countries, the Spanish peoples will reap the harvest not only of peace but of victory. Since, therefore, we are soon to fight a campaign in distant parts and nobody knows when you may see your homes and loved ones again, I have decided to grant leave of absence to any man who wishes to visit his family. Your orders are to return to duty at the beginning of spring, in order that, with God's help, we may begin a war which will fill your pockets with gold and carry your fame to the world's end.'

Most of the men were already feeling the separation from their families and looking forward sadly to a longer separation to come; so the unexpected offer of leave was very welcome. The whole winter was a time of inactivity between two periods of hard service, one completed, the other still to be faced, and the respite gave the troops fresh strength, both physical and moral, to endure again all that might be required of them. At the beginning of spring they reassembled according to orders.

After reviewing his auxiliary troops Hannibal went to Gades [Cadiz] to pay his vows to the Tyrian Hercules in the temple there, and swore to express further obligations to that god, should his affairs prosper. His next concern was the twofold task of perfecting his offensive and defensive measures. To obviate the danger of a Roman invasion of Africa by way of Sicily while he was marching for Italy through Spain and the Gallic provinces, he took the precaution of stationing a powerful force in the island. As this necessitated reinforcements, he asked for a fresh contingent of African troops, mostly light-armed spearmen, intending to employ African troops in Spain and Spanish troops in Africa in the belief that service by each in a foreign country would provide a sort of mutual guarantee of good behaviour. He sent 13,850 targeteers to Africa together with 870 slingers from the Balearic Islands and 1,200 cavalrymen of various nationality, some to serve in different parts of Africa, some to garrison Carthage; at the same time he dispatched officers to raise troops from the states dependent upon him, with orders that 4,000 picked men should be moved to Carthage to strengthen the garrison there and also to act as hostages. Spain moreover was not to be neglected, especially in view of the recent Roman attempt to seduce the leading men of the various Spanish peoples from their allegiance, and the defence of the country was put into the capable hands of his brother Hasdrubal. The troops under his command were mainly African: 11,850 African foot, 300 Ligurians, and 500 from the Balearics. To these were added 450 Libyphoenician horse – men of mixed blood, half Punic half African – about 1,800 Numidians and Moors from the Atlantic coast, and a small force of 200 horse from the Ilergetes in Spain.

Finally, there were twenty-one elephants, to make the land-forces complete. Furthermore, as it seemed likely that the Romans might attempt to repeat their former successes by sea, Hasdrubal was given for coastal defence a fleet of fifty quinquiremes, two quadriremes, and five triremes, though of these only thirty-two quinquiremes and five triremes were actually fitted out and manned.

From Gades Hannibal returned to the army's quarters in New Carthage, and then proceeded by way of Etovissa to the river Ebro and the coast. Here, the story goes, he had a dream: a young man of godlike aspect told him he had been sent by God to guide him to Italy, and bade him follow, and in all places keep his eyes fixed upon him. Conquering his fear, he followed the divine guide, looking neither to right nor left, nor behind, until overcome by a natural human curiosity and eager to know what it was he had been forbidden to see behind him, he was unable to control his eyes any longer. He looked round, and saw a monstrous snake, gliding; and in its path trees and bushes were tumbling in dreadful ruin, while a storm-cloud loomed up behind with the crash of thunder. He asked in his dream what that fearful commotion might be and what was the meaning of the sign, and a voice said in answer that it signified the laying waste of Italy, and that he must go forward without further questioning and allow what needs must be to remain in darkness.

Encouraged by his dream he proceeded to cross the Ebro, dividing his forces into three detachments. A party had already been sent ahead to Gaul with instructions to reconnoitre the Alpine passes and to endeavour to obtain by bribes the favour of the Gallic chieftains whose territories lay along the route the army would probably follow. The force with which he crossed the river amounted to 90,000 foot and 12,000 horse. The next objectives were the Iler-

getes, Bargusii, Ausetani, and the district of Laceta-
nia on the foothills of the Pyrenees; this whole
coastal area Hannibal put in charge of Hanno,
to keep control of the passes between the provinces of Spain and Gaul, assigning him a force of
10,000 infantry for the purpose. The march
through the passes of the Pyrenees then began.

By this time Hannibal's foreign troops had
become fairly sure of his ultimate objective – the
invasion of Italy; and as a result the contingent
from the Carpetani, 3,000 strong, refused to
proceed, in alarm, supposedly, less at the actual
prospect of the fighting than of the length of the
march and the well-nigh impossible passage of
the Alps. To recall the deserters or to detain
them by force might have adversely affected the
morale of his other foreign troops, wild and
undisciplined as they were, so Hannibal dismissed over 7,000 of his men whom he knew to
be resentful at the prospect of the campaign
ahead of them, and pretended that the deserters

had also been dismissed for the same reason. Then, to prevent the undermining of discipline by idleness and delay, he proceeded forthwith to cross the Pyrenees with the rest of his troops and encamped near the town of Iliberis.

The Gauls were aware that Italy was Hannibal's objective; nevertheless the news of the subjection of the Spanish peoples beyond the Pyrenees and the occupation of their country by a powerful force so alarmed them that, in fear of being themselves reduced to slavery, a number of their tribes flew to arms and concentrated at the town of Ruscino. Hannibal, to whom the only danger in this situation seemed to be a possible delay, sent a delegation to the Gallic chieftains with instructions to tell them that he desired a conference, for which purpose either he would advance to Ruscino, or they, if they preferred, could approach Iliberis, to facilitate a meeting. He would be glad to receive them in his own camp, or – alternatively – was equally willing to come to them without hesitation, as he had entered Gaul not as an enemy but as a friend and had no intention, unless they compelled him, of drawing the sword before he was in Italy. The message was duly delivered; the Gallic chieftains promptly moved with their men to Iliberis and were easily persuaded to meet Hannibal, whereupon the presents they received soon induced them to let the Carthaginian army move on past Ruscino and through their territory without molestation.

Meanwhile, before any news had reached Rome subsequent to the report of the envoys from Massilia that Hannibal had crossed the Ebro, the Boii incited their neighbours the Insubrian Gauls to join them in revolt – almost as if Hannibal were already over the Alps. The reason for their defection was not so much their long-standing hostility to Rome as resentment at the recent planting on Gallic soil of the two settlements of Placentia and Cremona, near the river

Po. Hurriedly mobilizing their forces they invaded that district and caused so much alarm and confusion that not only the rural population but even the three Roman officials who were superintending the assignment of land in the new settlement fled to Mutina, lest the walls of Placentia should prove an insufficient protection. The three officials were probably Gaius Lutatius, Gaius Servilius, and Titus Annius, though some annals have Quintus Acilius and Gaius Herennius in place of the two last, and others Publius Cornelius Asina and Gaius Papirius Maso. About Lutatius there is no discrepancy in the records. There is also some doubt about whether the envoys sent to demand reparations from the Boii were subjected to violence, or whether it was the three officials engaged upon the partition of agricultural land who were assaulted.

The Gauls were no great hands at military tactics and without any experience in siege warfare; against those shut up in Mutina they did nothing and no attempt was made to storm the defences. In these circumstances negotiations for a truce were opened – or so it was pretended. The Roman envoys, invited by the Gallic chiefs to a conference, were seized – an action which violated not only the accepted conventions of international procedure but also the specific guarantees given on the occasion – and the Gauls refused to release them unless their hostages were restored.

At the news of the envoys' plight and of the danger to Mutina and its garrison, the praetor Lucius Manlius started for the town with a relief-party. Indignation prevented proper precautions being taken. Most of the neighbourhood was uncultivated, and his road lay through woods. He had no scouts out, and the result was that he fell into a trap and suffered severe losses before he managed to struggle clear into open country. There he halted, and properly fortified his position; and his men, in spite of their losses – probably some 500 killed – recovered their morale when they found that the enemy seemed to have no heart for a concerted attack. They proceeded on their way, and so long as their route led through open country, there was no further sign of the enemy; once again, however, the moment they got into woodland, the rear of the column was attacked. Discipline went to pieces, and panic spread; six standards were lost and 700 men killed. It was not till the force emerged from the trackless and difficult wooded country that the Gauls stopped their alarming tactics and the Roman column could breathe freely. Thereafter, marching through open country, they had no difficulty in protecting themselves, and proceeded to Tannetum, a village near the Po, where they temporarily fortified a position. This, together with such provisions as could be brought down the river and the assistance of the Brixian Gauls, kept them in comparative safety against the daily increasing numbers of the enemy.

In Rome the report of this unexpected trouble, and the knowledge that the Roman government now had a war with Gaul as well as with Carthage on its hands, called for prompt action. The Senate ordered fresh troops to be raised, and instructed the praetor Gaius Atilius to march to Manlius's relief with one Roman legion and 5,000 allied troops. The enemy having dispersed in alarm, the force reached Tannetum unmolested.

At the same time Cornelius Scipio, having raised a fresh legion in place of the one which had been ordered out with the praetor, sailed from Rome with sixty warships. Coasting Etruria and Liguria, he went on past the mountains of the Salyes until he reached Massilia, where he established himself on the easternmost of the several mouths of the Rhône. He was not yet by any means sure that Hannibal had crossed the

Pyrenees, though he was soon to learn that he was already preparing to cross the Rhône. As he did not know where he was likely to make contact with him, and his men had not yet recovered from the effects of their rough voyage, he took the precaution of sending out a reconnoitring party of 300 mounted troops, with local guides and supported by a Gallic contingent, to find out all they could and to watch the enemy's movements without risking an encounter. Hannibal had by now reached the territory of the Volcae, having either scared or bribed the other tribes into submission. The Volcae were a powerful people with settlements on both banks of the Rhône, but as they distrusted their ability to keep the Carthaginians from reaching the river they had decided to make use of it as a barrier to their further advance. With this in view nearly all of them had crossed over and were now holding the farther, or eastern, bank. The other tribes in the neighbourhood of the river, and even such men of the Volcae who had not abandoned their homes, Hannibal induced by the offer of presents to construct boats and rafts and to collect others from wherever they could find them. The natives themselves were only too eager to see Hannibal safely across and to have their own territory relieved as quickly as possible from the burden of his numerous army; so it was not long before an immense number of craft was assembled, big and small – the latter roughly-built boats for local use, while at the same time the Gauls set about constructing canoes hollowed from a single tree-trunk. The Carthaginian soldiers soon followed suit. The work was easy and timber abundant, and, as the only requirement was something that would float and carry a load, the result was the rapid construction of a number of rough and more or less shapeless hulls, which would at least take them and their gear across the river.

As soon as preparations were complete, they

were deterred from proceeding by an assembly in force of the enemy, both horse and foot, who were thronging the farther bank of the river. To circumvent this menace, Hannibal sent Hanno, the son of Bomilcar, with a party of men, mostly Spanish, a day's journey up the river; his instructions were to start soon after dark and, on the first opportunity, to cross over, attracting as little attention as possible, and then, by an outflanking movement, to attack the enemy in the rear when occasion offered. Information was given by the Gallic guides that some twenty-five miles upstream there was a convenient place for crossing, where the river was broader and shallower as it was split into two channels by a small island. Timber was quickly cut and rafts constructed to carry the men over, together with their horses and gear, the Spanish troops making no bones about swimming across with their shields beneath them and their clothes stowed in leather bags. The rest of the force crossed on the rafts, lashed together to form a bridge. Camp was then pitched near the river bank, and the men were given a day's rest to recover from their night march and subsequent labours, their commanding officer being anxious to avoid any sort of miscarriage in the operation. Next day they got on the move again, and raised a smoke signal to indicate that they were across the river and not far away. Hannibal saw the signal, and gave immediate orders for his own men to begin their passage of the river. For the infantrymen the boats were already prepared; most of the cavalry was got across with the men swimming by the side of their horses, a line of larger craft being stationed just above them to break the force of the current, and to make easier going for the rafts and boats farther downstream. Many of the horses were attached by lines to boats' sterns, while the rest were ferried across ready saddled and bridled, for instant use by their riders on the farther side.

The Gallic warriors came surging to the river bank, howling and singing as their custom was, shaking their shields above their heads and brandishing their spears, in spite of the menace which confronted them of those innumerable hostile craft, rendered yet more alarming by the roar of the stream and the cries of the soldiers and sailors struggling to overcome the fierce current and the shouts of encouragement from their comrades awaiting their turn to cross. All this was bad enough; but suddenly, from behind, a more terrible sound assailed their ears – the triumphant shout of Hanno's men. Their camp had been captured, and a moment later Hanno himself was upon them: they were caught between two deadly menaces, the thousands of armed men landing on the river bank and a second army unexpectedly pressing upon their rear. After one fruitless attempt at active resistance they forced a way out of the trap as best they could and dispersed in confusion to their villages. Hannibal, now convinced that there was more smoke than fire in Gallic resistance, completed at leisure the passage of the river, and pitched camp.

Various methods were, I believe, employed to get the elephants across; at any rate there are differing accounts of how it was done. According to one account, the beasts were herded close to the bank, and a notably ferocious one was then goaded by his driver, who promptly plunged into the water; the furious animal pursued him as he swam for his life and so drew the rest of the herd after him. Despite their terror at finding themselves in deep water, they were all carried to the farther bank by the sheer force of the current. It is more generally thought that they were ferried across on rafts – surely a safer method, and also, to judge by the result, a more likely one. The method was to prepare a big float, 200 feet long and 50 feet wide, which was held in position against the current by a number of strong cables which led to the bank upstream; it was then covered with soil like a bridge, to induce the elephants to walk on to it without fear, as if they were still on land. To this float a second raft, of the same width but only half the length, and suitable for towing across the river, was attached. The elephants, the females leading, were driven on to the float – supposing it to be a solid road – and then passed on to the raft, when the ropes which lightly attached it to the float were immediately cast off, and it was towed over to the farther bank by rowing-boats. When the first batch had been landed, others were fetched and brought over. None of the animals showed any alarm so long as they were on what seemed the solid bridge: panic began only when the raft was cast off and they found themselves being carried into deep water; it was then that they showed fright, those nearest the edge backing away from the water and causing much jostling and confusion amongst their companions, until their very terror, at the sight of water all around them, seemed to freeze them into stillness. A few completely lost their heads and fell into the water; their riders were flung off, but the beasts themselves, stabilized by their weight, struggled on bit by bit till they found shallow water, and so got ashore.

While this operation was in progress, Hannibal had sent a party of 500 Numidian horsemen to try to find out the location, strength, and intentions of the Roman force. The Numidians were met by the party of 300 Roman cavalrymen, who had been sent, as I have already mentioned, from the mouth of the Rhône to reconnoitre. The fight which followed was, in spite of the small numbers engaged, a surprisingly savage one; many were wounded and the losses in killed were about equal on both sides. It was only when the Romans had already had nearly enough that the Numidians broke and fled, and so gave them the victory. Roman losses, including the Gallic auxiliaries, amounted to 160; those of the Numidians to over 200. This preliminary skirmish might be taken as an omen of what was to come – portending final victory for Rome, but at the same time a victory far from bloodless and won only after a struggle of which the issue was to be long in doubt.

When the troops returned after this engagement to their respective commanders, Scipio could be sure of only one thing, namely that he must adjust his own movements to the actions and strategy of the enemy. Hannibal, for his part, was still hesitating between continuing his march straight into Italy, and offering battle to the first Roman force that chanced to lie in his way; he was, however, dissuaded from an immediate trial of strength with Scipio by the arrival of a delegation from the Boii with their chieftain Magulas, who promised to serve him as guides and to share his dangers, at the same time expressing the opinion that the invasion of

Italy should be his sole objective, to be undertaken without any frittering away of his strength.

The rank and file of the Carthaginian army had a wholesome respect for Roman arms, as the former war was not yet forgotten; but they were much more alarmed by the prospect of the long march and, especially, of the passage of the Alps – about which stories were told dreadful enough to frighten anyone, particularly the inexperienced. In view of this, Hannibal, once he had made his decision to go ahead and to make straight for Italy, paraded his troops and delivered an address calculated to work upon their feelings by a judicious mixture of reproof and encouragement. 'What sudden panic is this,' he said, 'which has entered those breasts where fear has never been? Year after year you have fought with me, and won; and you never left Spain until all the lands and peoples between the two seas were subject to our power. When the Roman people demanded the surrender of the "criminal" – whoever it might have been – who laid siege to Saguntum, you were justly angry and crossed the Ebro bent upon obliterating the very name of Rome and setting the world free. Then, at least, none of you thought of the journey long, though it stretched from the setting to the rising sun; but now, when you can see that much the greater part of the distance is already behind you – when you have made your way through the wild tribes and over the passes of the Pyrenees, when you have tamed the violence of the mighty Rhône and crossed it in face of those countless Gallic warriors who would fain have stopped you; when, finally, you have the Alps in sight, and know that the other side of them is Italian soil: now, I repeat, at the very gateway of the enemy's country, you come to a halt – exhausted! What do you think the Alps *are*? Are they anything worse than high mountains? Say, if you will, that they are higher than the Pyrenees, but what of it? No part of earth reaches the sky; no height is insuperable to men. Moreover, the Alps are not desert: men live there, they till the ground; there are animals there, living creatures. If a small party can cross them, surely armies can? The envoys you see with us did not, in order to get over, soar into the air on wings. Moreover, their own forebears were immigrants – they were countryfolk from Italy, who often crossed these same mountains safely enough – hordes of them, with their women and children, whole peoples on the move. Surely, then, for an army of soldiers, with nothing to carry but their military gear, no waste should be too wild to cross, no hills too high to climb. Remember Saguntum, and those eight long months of toil and peril endured to the end. It is not Saguntum now, but Rome, the mightiest city of the world, you aim to conquer: how can you feel that anything, however hard, however dangerous, can make you hesitate?

Why, even the Gauls once captured Rome – and you despair of being able even to get near it. Either confess, then, you have less spirit and courage than a people you have again and again defeated during these latter days, or steel your hearts to march forward, to halt only on Mars' Field between the Tiber and the walls of Rome.'

Hannibal's words were not without effect. When he had ended, he gave the order for his men to rest and prepare themselves for the march.

The army moved on the following day. The route Hannibal chose was along the Rhône valley towards central Gaul. This was not the more direct route to the Alps. But Hannibal preferred it as the farther he got from the coast the less likely he was to encounter Roman resistance, and he had no wish for a trial of strength until he reached Italy. Four days later he was at the junction of the Isaras and the Rhône, both of which flow down from the Alps and embrace a stretch of country known as the Island. In this neighbourhood was the territory of the Allobroges, a people even in those days inferior to none in Gaul for power and fame. At the time of Hannibal's arrival the country was split by internal discord, two brothers disputing for the throne; the elder, Brancus, had been king, but an attempt was being made by his younger brother to depose him, with the support of the young nobles and the claim that might, in this case, was right. The two rivals seized the opportunity of Hannibal's presence to refer to him the decision of the quarrel, and he, acting as arbitrator, and supporting the views of the council and the leading men, restored the throne of Brancus. In recognition of this service he was assisted by a gift of provisions and supplies of all sorts, especially of clothing, which it was essential to lay in against the notorious cold of the high Alps.

The business of the Allobroges settled, Hannibal's objective was now the mountains themselves.

Still avoiding the most direct route, he turned left to the territory of the Tricastini, proceeding thence past the borders of the Vocontii to the Tricorii and finding nothing to stop him until he reached the river Druentia [River Drôme]. This Alpine stream is more awkward to cross than any other river in Gaul; in spite of its volume of water nothing can float on it, because, not being contained by banks, it is split up into a number of constantly changing channels, where the shallows and deep potholes, dangerous to a man on foot, shift from day to day; add the stones and gravel swept down by the rapid current, and it is clear that anyone who enters will find a foothold by no means firm or safe. On this occasion the stream was swollen by rains, with the result that the crossing was a scene of extraordinary confusion, the rank and file adding to the very real and actual dangers by their own disorderly clamour and desperate haste to get over.

The consul Publius Cornelius had reached

Hannibal's position on the Rhône three days too late. His troops were in battle order, and his intention was to engage immediately; but all he found was an empty encampment. As it became clear to him that Hannibal had too long a start to be easily overtaken, he rejoined his fleet, thinking that the better and safer course would be to confront Hannibal on his descent of the Alps into northern Italy. At the same time, as he was unwilling to leave his own province of Spain without a Roman force to protect it, he sent the greater part of his army there under the command of his brother Gnaeus Scipio, with instructions not only to support against Hasdrubal the Spanish peoples who were already friendly to Rome and to win others to her alliance, but also, if he could, to drive Hasdrubal from Spain altogether. He himself meanwhile returned with quite a small force to Genoa intending to defend Italy with the troops already stationed in the vicinity of the Po.

From the Druentia Hannibal advanced towards the Alps mainly through open country, and reached the foothills without encountering any opposition from the local tribes. The nature of the mountains was not, of course, unknown to his men by rumour and report – and rumour commonly exaggerates the truth; yet in this case all tales were eclipsed by the reality. The dreadful vision was now before their eyes: the towering peaks, the snow-clad pinnacles soaring to the sky, the rude huts clinging to the rocks, beasts and cattle shrivelled and parched with cold, the people with their wild and ragged hair, all nature, animate and inanimate, stiff with frost: all this, and other sights the horror of which words cannot express, gave a fresh edge to their apprehension. As the column moved forward up the first slopes, there appeared, right above their heads, ensconced upon their eminences, the local tribesmen, wild men of the mountains, who, if they had chosen to lurk in clefts of the hills, might well have sprung out from ambush upon the marching column and inflicted untold losses and disaster.

Hannibal soon ordered a halt and sent his Gallic guides forward to reconnoitre. Informed that he could not get through here, he encamped in the best stretch of fairly level ground he could find, hemmed in though it was by savagely broken rocks and precipitous cliffs. Later he learned from the same guides, whose way of life and language were much like those of the local tribesmen, and who had been able, in consequence, to listen to their deliberations, that the pass was held only in the daytime, and that at nightfall the natives dispersed to their homes. In view of this information, at dawn next morning he approached the eminences where the tribesmen were on watch as if with the intention of openly trying to force a passage through the defile during the hours of daylight. During the rest of the day he concealed his actual purpose;

his men fortified the position where they had originally halted, and it was not till he was sure that the tribesmen had abandoned the heights and gone off guard that his real intention became evident. Leaving the baggage in camp with all the cavalry and most of the infantry, and kindling, for a blind, more fires than the numbers actually left in camp would justify, he assembled a force of light-armed infantrymen, all men picked for their courage and determination, swiftly cleared the defile, and established himself on the heights which the tribesmen had been holding. At dawn next morning camp was broken up and the rest of the army moved forward.

The tribesmen were beginning to muster at their usual look-out station on the heights when, to their astonishment, they saw the Carthaginian assault-troops right above their heads and already in possession of it, while another army of them was passing through along the track. The two things together were such a shock to them that for the moment they were frozen into immobility; soon, however, the sight of the enemy's own difficulties restored their confidence. In the narrow pass the marching column was rapidly losing cohesion; there was great confusion and excitement amongst the men, and still more amongst the terrified horses, so the tribesmen, in the hope that any hostile action by themselves would be enough to complete their discomfiture, came swarming down the rocky and precipitous slopes, sure-footed as they were from long familiarity with their wild and trackless terrain. The Carthaginians thus found themselves facing two enemies – the hostile tribesmen and the terrible difficulty of their position in the narrow defile. It was a case of every man for himself, and in their struggles to get clear of danger they were fighting with each other rather than with the enemy. It was the horses, more than anything else, which created havoc in the column: terrified by the din, echoing and re-echoing from the hollow cliffs and woods, they were soon out of control, while those which were struck or wounded lashed out in an agony of fear, causing serious losses both of men and gear of all descriptions. In the confusion many non-combatants, and not a few soldiers, were flung over the sheer cliffs which bounded each side of the pass, and fell to their deaths thousands of feet below; but it was worst for the pack-animals – loads and all, they went tumbling over the edge almost like falling masonry.

All this was a shocking spectacle; nevertheless Hannibal, watching from above, stayed for the moment where he was and kept his assault-troops in check, lest their joining the column should only add to the confusion. But when he saw the column break up, and realized that even to get the men through safely would not help him much if all their gear were lost, he knew it was time to act. Hurrying down from his position on the heights, he scattered the hostile tribesmen with a single charge. His arrival did, indeed, increase the confusion amongst his own men, but only for a moment; for once the enemy had fled and the track was clear, order was restored, and it was not long before the whole army, unmolested and almost in silence, was brought safely through. The chief fortified village of the district, together with the neighbouring hamlets, was then captured, and the cattle and grain taken from these places proved sufficient to feed the army for three days. As the tribesmen had learnt their lesson, and the going was now comparatively easy, the army during these three days made considerable progress.

Coming to the territory of another mountain tribe, a numerous one for this sort of country, Hannibal encountered no open resistance, but fell into a cunningly laid trap. In fact he nearly succumbed to the very tactics in which he himself excelled. The elders of the fortified villages presented themselves in the guise of envoys, and declared that the wholesome example of others' suffering had taught them to prefer the friendship of the Carthaginians to the risk of learning at first hand of their military might. They were willing, in consequence, to submit to Hannibal's orders, to supply him with guides and provisions, and to offer hostages as a guarantee of their good faith. Hannibal was too cautious to take what they said at its face value, but was unwilling to reject the offer out of hand, lest a refusal should drive them into open hostility; accordingly he replied in friendly terms, accepted the hostages, and made use of the supplies the natives had offered; he then followed their guides – but with proper precautions, and by no means proceeding in loose order, as he might have done in friendly territory.

At the head of the column were the cavalry and elephants; Hannibal himself, with the pick of the infantry, brought up the rear, keeping his eyes open and alert for every contingency. Before long the column found itself on a narrowing track, one side of which was overhung by a precipitous wall of rock, and it was suddenly attacked. The natives, springing from their places of concealment, fiercely assaulted front and rear, leaping into the fray, hurling missiles, rolling down rocks from the heights above. The worst pressure was on Hannibal's rear; to meet it, his infantry faced-about – and it was clear enough that, had not the rear of the column been adequately protected, the Carthaginian losses would have been appalling. Even as it was the moment was critical, and disaster only just averted; for Hannibal hesitated to send his own division into the pass – to do so would have deprived the infantry of such support as he was himself providing for the cavalry – and his hesitation enabled the tribesmen to deliver a flank attack, cut the whole column in two, and establish themselves on the track. As a result,

Hannibal, for one night, found himself cut off from his cavalry and baggage-train. Next day, however, as enemy activity weakened, a junction was effected between the two halves of the column and the defile was successfully passed, though not without losses, especially amongst the pack-animals.

Thenceforward there was no concerted opposition, the natives confining themselves to mere raids, in small parties, on front or rear, as the nature of the ground dictated, or as groups of stragglers, left behind or pressing on ahead of the column as the case might be, offered a tempting prey. The elephants proved both a blessing and a curse: for though getting them along the narrow and precipitous tracks caused serious delay, they were none the less a protection to the troops, as the natives, never having seen such creatures before, were afraid to come near them.

On the ninth day the army reached the

summit. Most of the climb had been over track-less mountain-sides; frequently a wrong route was taken – sometimes through the deliberate deception of the guides, or, again, when some likely-looking valley would be entered by guess-work, without knowledge of whither it led. There was a two days' halt on the summit, to rest the men after the exhausting climb and the fighting. Some of the pack-animals which had fallen amongst the rocks managed, by following the army's tracks, to find their way into camp. The troops had indeed endured hardships enough; but there was worse to come. It was the season of the setting of the Pleiades [late October]: winter was near – and it began to snow. Getting on the move at dawn, the army struggled slowly forward over snow-covered ground, the hopelessness of utter exhaustion in every face. Seeing their despair, Hannibal rode ahead and at a point of vantage which afforded a prospect of a vast extent of country, he gave the order to halt, pointing to Italy far below, and the Po Valley beyond the foothills of the Alps. 'My men,' he said, 'you are at this moment passing the protective barrier of Italy – nay more, you are walking over the very walls of Rome. Henceforward all will be easy going – no more hills to climb. After a fight or two you will have the capital of Italy, the citadel of Rome, in the hollow of your hands.'

The march continued, more or less without molestation from the natives, who confined themselves to petty raids when they saw a chance of stealing something. Unfortunately, however, as in most parts of the Alps the descent on the Italian side, being shorter, is correspondingly steeper, the going was much more difficult than it had been during the ascent. The track was almost everywhere precipitous, narrow, and slippery; it was impossible for a man to keep his feet; the least stumble meant a fall, and a fall a slide, so that there was indescribable confusion, men and beasts stumbling and slipping on top of each other.

Soon they found themselves on the edge of a precipice – a narrow cliff falling away so sheer that even a lightly-armed soldier could hardly have got down it by feeling his way and clinging to such bushes and stumps as presented themselves. It must always have been a most awkward spot, but a recent landslide had converted it on this occasion to a perpendicular drop of nearly a thousand feet. On the brink the cavalry drew rein – their journey seemed to be over. Hannibal, in the rear, did not yet know what had brought the column to a halt; but when the message was passed to him that there was no possibility of proceeding, he went in person to reconnoitre. It was clear to him that a detour would have to be made, however long it might prove to be, over the trackless and untrodden slopes in the vicinity. But even so he was no luckier; progress was impossible, for though there was good foothold in the quite shallow layer of soft fresh snow which had covered the old snow underneath, nevertheless as soon as it had been trampled and dispersed by the feet of all those men and animals, there was left to tread upon only the bare ice and liquid slush of melting snow underneath. The result was a horrible struggle, the ice affording no foothold in any case, and least of all on a steep slope; when a man tried by hands or knees to get on his feet again, even those useless supports slipped from under him and let him down; there were no stumps or roots anywhere to afford a purchase to either foot or hand; in short, there was nothing for it but to roll and slither on the smooth ice and melting snow. Sometimes the mules' weight would drive their hoofs through into the lower layer of old snow; they would fall and, once down, lashing savagely out in their struggles to rise, they would break right through it, so that as often as not they were held as in a vice by a thick layer of hard ice.

When it became apparent that both men and beasts were wearing themselves out to no purpose, a space was cleared – with the greatest labour because of the amount of snow to be dug and carted away – and camp was pitched, high up on the ridge. The next task was to construct some sort of passable track down the precipice, for by no other route could the army proceed. It was necessary to cut through rock, a problem they solved by the ingenious application of heat and moisture; large trees were felled and lopped, and a huge pile of timber erected; this, with the opportune help of a strong wind, was set on fire, and when the rock was sufficiently heated the men's rations of sour wine were flung upon it, to render it friable. They then got to work with picks on the heated rock, and opened a sort of zigzag track, to minimize the steepness of the descent, and were able, in consequence, to get the pack animals, and even the elephants, down it.

Four days were spent in the neighbourhood of this precipice; the animals came near to dying of starvation, for on most of the peaks nothing grows, or, if there is any pasture, the snow covers it. Lower down there are sunny hills and valleys and woods with streams flowing by: country, in fact, more worthy for men to dwell in. There the beasts were put out to pasture, and the troops given three days' rest to recover from the fatigue of their road-building. Thence the descent was continued to the plains – a kindlier region, with kindlier inhabitants.

The march to Italy was much as I have described it. The army reached the frontier in the fifth month, as some records have it, after leaving New Carthage. The crossing of the Alps took fifteen days.

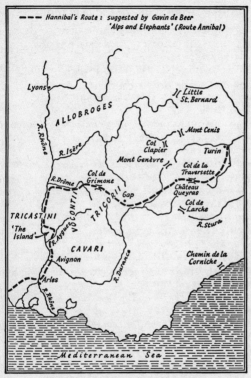

Hannibal's crossing of the Alps

45

PENGUIN 60s CLASSICS

PENGUIN 60s CLASSICS

ANONYMOUS WORKS

READ MORE IN PENGUIN

For complete information about books available from Penguin and how to order them, please write to us at the appropriate address below. Please note that for copyright reasons the selection of books varies from country to country.

IN THE UNITED KINGDOM: Please write to *Dept. JC, Penguin Books Ltd, FREEPOST, West Drayton, Middlesex UB7 0BR*.

If you have any difficulty in obtaining a title, please send your order with the correct money, plus ten per cent for postage and packaging, to *PO Box No. 11, West Drayton, Middlesex UB7 0BR*.

IN THE UNITED STATES: Please write to *Consumer Sales, Penguin USA, P.O. Box 999, Dept. 17109, Bergenfield, New Jersey 07621-0120*. VISA and MasterCard holders call 1-800-253-6476 to order all Penguin titles.

IN CANADA: Please write to *Penguin Books Canada Ltd, 10 Alcorn Avenue, Suite 300, Toronto, Ontario M4V 3B2*.

IN AUSTRALIA: Please write to *Penguin Books Australia Ltd, P.O. Box 257, Ringwood, Victoria 3134*.

IN NEW ZEALAND: Please write to *Penguin Books (NZ) Ltd, Private Bag 102902, North Shore Mail Centre, Auckland 10*.

IN INDIA: Please write to *Penguin Books India Pvt Ltd, 706 Eros Apartments, 56 Nehru Place, New Delhi 110 019*.

IN THE NETHERLANDS: Please write to *Penguin Books Netherlands bv, Postbus 3507, NL-1001 AH Amsterdam*.

IN GERMANY: Please write to *Penguin Books Deutschland GmbH, Metzlerstrasse 26, 60594 Frankfurt am Main*.

IN SPAIN: Please write to *Penguin Books S. A., Bravo Murillo 19, 1° B, 28015 Madrid*.

IN ITALY: Please write to *Penguin Italia s.r.l., Via Felice Casati 20, I-20124 Milano*.

IN FRANCE: Please write to *Penguin France S. A., 17 rue Lejeune, F-31000 Toulouse*.

IN JAPAN: Please write to *Penguin Books Japan, Ishikiribashi Building, 2-5-4, Suido, Bunkyo-ku, Tokyo 112*.

IN GREECE: Please write to *Penguin Hellas Ltd, Dimocritou 3, GR-106 71 Athens*.

IN SOUTH AFRICA: Please write to *Longman Penguin Southern Africa (Pty) Ltd Private Bag X08, Bertsham 2013*.